PRAISE FOR

Sparrow

Sparrow demonstrates that the requiem, the elegy and the blues are not always primal cries of hopelessness and despair, but are—at their most sublime—enduring efforts to turn that which is deeply devastating into something beautiful, even transcendent. *Sparrow*'s understated musicality, intelligent architecture, and naked honesty seduce and comfort, even as the poems guide us through the pain of death, the details of marital disquiet, and the grace of marital love. Whether she is employing classical or contemporary forms, Muske-Dukes is teaching us how to grieve and lament, all over again.
—The National Book Foundation

"The poet's voice here is not so much the sob of grief as the measured tones of one who has long since run out of tears. . . . Anyone who has suffered a great loss—or who has lived through a marriage, with all its daily deaths of mutual understanding—will be able to relate to the blunt emotions here."
—*Time Out New York*

"[Muske-Dukes] is a highly lyrical poet who knows how to sing with the best of them. . . . [*Sparrow*] shines."
—*Rocky Mountain News*

"Longing and grief produce concentrated moments of terse, wry observations on grief. . . . Heartbreaking."
—*Publishers Weekly*

"Seductive . . . These are lovely, artful meditations—a profound elegy to the man [Muske-Dukes] still loves."
—*Deseret Morning News*

"While it is deeply personal, *Sparrow* is also an intricate marriage of dramatic and lyric voices, grief so acutely rendered it prefigures centuries of love and loss."   —TheStranger.com (Seattle)

"Marriage is a pact with an other both beloved and unknowable—and loss, therefore, means losing both what we know and what we can never circumscribe. *Sparrow* is a stunning elegy for the actor David Dukes, but like all great poetry, it reaches beyond the specifics of a life, or a death. In poems haunted by Lear and Godot, Catullus and Oscar Wilde, a chorus of shades, art's animating phantoms, ghost this brooding, loving book into startling life."   —MARK DOTY

"*Sparrow* is an act of retrieval, a way of reviving David Dukes through memory. The lines of the poems are, in effect, life-lines, and within them he is brought back in a second life, one that will last."   —MARK STRAND

CAROL MUSKE-DUKES is the founder and director of the graduate program in literature and creative writing at the University of Southern California. Her last collection of poetry, *An Octave Above Thunder*, was nominated for the *Los Angeles Times* Book Prize, and she has been the recipient of many awards, among them a Guggenheim fellowship. She has written three novels, and *Married to the Icepick Killer*, a collection of essays on Hollywood and poetry published in 2002 and named a Best Book of 2002 by the *San Francisco Chronicle*, is her most recent book. She writes a regular column for the *Los Angeles Times Book Review* called "Poets' Corner" and reviews for *The New York Times*. Muske-Dukes lives in Los Angeles with her daughter.

Sparrow was a National Book Award nominee for 2003.

www.carolmuskedukes.com

ALSO BY CAROL MUSKE-DUKES

POETRY (as Carol Muske)
Camouflage
Skylight
Wyndmere
Applause
Red Trousseau
An Octave Above Thunder

FICTION
Dear Digby
Saving St. Germ
Life After Death

ESSAYS
Women and Poetry: Truth, Autobiography, and the Shape of the Self
Married to the Icepick Killer: A Poet in Hollywood

Sparrow

Sparrow

POEMS

CAROL MUSKE-DUKES

RANDOM HOUSE TRADE PAPERBACKS

NEW YORK

Some of the poems in this book have been previously
published in the following magazines: "A Private Matter," *The
New Yorker;* "Love Song," *Poetry* (ninetieth-anniversary issue);
"Portrait," "Valli," *TriQuarterly;* "The Illusion," "Ovation,"
The Yale Review; "Magnificat," *The New Republic;* "Ionic," "Not
for Burning," "Waiting For," "Like You," "Studio City,"
American Poetry Review; "Late Kiss," *O: The Oprah Magazine;*
"Actor," "Heart," "Anniversary," *The Kenyon Review;* "Choice,"
"Le Jazz Hot," *Cavankerry Anthology;* "The Queen of Tragedy,"
"The Machine," "When He Fell," *Slate* (on-line); "Players,"
"Blue Morpho," *Ploughshares;* "Strange Interlude," "The
Empty Chair," "Box," *Gulf Coast;* "Passport: a Manifesto," *The
Nation.*
    "The Call" and "When He Fell" were broadcast on *Fresh
Air* on National Public Radio.

Library of Congress Cataloging-in-Publication Data
Muske-Dukes, Carol.
    Sparrow : poems / Carol Muske-Dukes.
        p.   cm.
    ISBN 0-8129-6748-8
        I. Title.
    PS3563.U837 S68   2003
    811'.54—dc21   2002035689

For David Coleman Dukes
1945–2000

There's a special providence in the fall of a sparrow.

—Hamlet, V.ii

CONTENTS

VALENTINE'S DAY, 2003

By the heart, the heart is shaped for use.
Sweet Valentine, think on thy Proteus.

Heart and shaper of the heart.
One a swift violent muscle,
the other pure impetus: digitalis

of metaphor setting the changing
pace. Steady waves on the hospital chart
    or *a spin in Death's speedboat*—

Consider the dangerous white wake
           in which we surface.
Wish me partake in thy happiness
When thou dost meet good hap

The first plane flies into the building.
The second into the heart's history.
And in thy danger
If ever danger do environ thee

Your death and the world's dying
seem, to me, one. Bomb strapped on
the chest, left side. A man stepping off a lit deck
                    into singing air.

Commend thy grievance to my holy prayers
For I was the one you loved

though each act of terror took away
the perspective of measured breath.

For I will be thy beadsman, Valentine
Beadsman now and this beating heart—
as the speedboat turns back across its own churning wake.
Terror and love, word & gesture, our hap. This sweet awful day.
This valentine.

Sparrow

IONIC

—after Cavafy

That their statues are broken,
that their temples are empty
doesn't mean that they are dead, the gods.

The gods never die—but memory
clears itself like the sky over Ionia—
Ionia the dream that is always forgotten
at dawn. The eyes of the god, the upturned

eyes, take in everything, nothing escapes
that gaze—then it is all enveloped in fire,
invisible fire of waking, the shudder of
returning consciousness, the lit blades.

But once I caught the winged figure, indistinct,
ascending. I saw him turn back and stare at me,
not able to erase what he knew I'd seen. His eyes
implicated in the loss, sudden pathos—then disappearance
$\qquad\qquad\qquad\qquad$ over the bright hills.

WAITING FOR

Was I sleeping, while the others suffered?
You asked, because you were Vladimir
And it was your turn to speak, to cry out
Astride the grave, a difficult birth . . .

Then I was terrified of you and your
transient's heart, your hat pulled down
to your eyes, bewhiskered, old—your
gaze young, demented, blue. It occurred

to me that we'd never come to a crossroads.
Or we'd always come to a crossroads. The
two tramps were waiting, but we never
waited for each other. Habit is a great

deadener, Vladimir said, but we never
lived with habit. You sat up in bed,
you howled as I philosophized, your face alight.
Leaves fell upward. We laughed, weightless,

pulled down by gravity. Each day was unlike
the others. For years at a time, years at
a time, remember? Or not.
Nothing in our lives was ever usual.

Every spark of likelihood has gone
as Jennet said. The morning came and
went, but you did not appear: a messenger
on some official errand of compassion,
catching you up in its aura of shy nobility.

If likelihood has gone, then let unlikeness
take the place of all I know for certain.
There were battles fought here but blood has
dried in patterns so aberrative it appears

now that we are in a painting of a war.
We await the mad ambulance driver
who sped recklessly all night with those
he saved from what had already happened—

precious stolen cargo heading toward
willing suspension, our shining dis-
animated sanctuary. They say light
set out early in pursuit—wanting to

claim each face, victorious—stupidly
refusing to admit defeat, shade by shade,
as if my tender headlong painted night
wouldn't let up be down, left right,

as if no one could ever die, or die
of this, this dream-sick recruitless longing.

I could not lie like you
among blossoms
and paper butterflies.
I could not offer my body
to the flames as you did.

Though now I was calm,
irrevocably harmed.
Feeling myself embraced,
I tried to offer no resistance
to life, its unbearable affections.

In fact,
I took to death naturally
and death took to me.
Death was a critic, like me.
Death could never be the actor—
rather the one standing by, waiting to
interpret, to predict, waiting to re-phrase
what has already been said perfectly,
the man whispering to the woman,
the child crying then laughing, the mouth drawing
                its last breath: opening, then closing.

WHEN HE FELL

When he fell, strangers ran to him.
Strangers called for help, lifted
his body and carried it. Then strangers
cut him, emptied him. Their ideas

of death determined when I would
touch him again. Their ideas of death
closed door after door between us,
altered his face, altered his presence—

violated the contract, the marriage,
took away even his wounded heart.
When he was at last delivered to me,
I was no longer myself—just as he

no longer had a self. They
had taken everything from us. Authority—
everywhere I turned. Just as he and I
once thought we were authorities over

our own lives, our work, our sense of
mortality, imagination—oh, and that
"sense of loss" that predicated everything—
you know, what we called *our personal lives*.

ACTOR

You give me up
You go away
You walk on a stage
and are re-made.

I long for you
but you have a strophic
relationship to longing.

You move so gracefully
between what the author intended,
what the audience requires.

Perfect messenger, you want nothing.
You never wanted more than that
annunciatory light on your face,

the words learned by heart so that the body
could make every human intention inviolable.
All is revelation in that world, how could I

have ever competed with such implacable
possession of gesture? When you crossed under
the arc of the proscenium, you were already dead

to me, yet more alive than ever. You turned back
once to look at me over your shoulder, opening the Stage
Door. Not yet made up, but already a stranger, the hawk
                              staring out of your face.

HEART

To you, joking, I'd said: *You're an actor.*
Act like you love me. You laughed and turned
away into the characters you played, acting like
an actor. We were caught in the force field,

the imagination's need for analogy, the analogy's
need for identity. Identity meant self-rescue by
definition though its fierce assumption forged a link,
a twinned longing we'd never admitted between

us, just below the surface of our lives. Something
woke me, night after night—insistent, reverberant—a word
finally understood outside conjuncture: *heart.* Instead of turning
to you, breathing next to me in the bed, I put my hand on my own

chest, my own pulse. I listened to the hurried beats—thought, afraid,
about the moving phrase of light on the wall that I could not, at that time,
begin to decipher.

THE MACHINE

Night after night when he was young,
he told me, he dreamed the same dream.
It was not a simple dream, the machine.

At first it half-coalesced as a drill press
or lathe, a thing that controlled the direction
of force to alter shape. Parts turned: ratchets,

gears, bearings. The machine in his troubled sleep
was a series of perfectable gestures in the spirit of
the cam-shaft: a projection on a rotating part

shaped to engender motion—but was not erotic exactly.
The machine was the point at which the lever was placed
to gain purchase, the fulcrum, the means by which influence

is brought to bear, the chime of iron against iron in a black rack,
power against resistance. What was its purpose as he perfected
it each night? Not to assemble or sort or tattoo patterns on metal.

It shimmered, a thousand lit pins, a system—a series of moving
parts that would never still, synchronous. What would it
replace? The erratic—manufactured as a strap—a father lashing

a son into a place of dark stasis. Standing up to audition, he had
the words at last, he'd gotten his mind round the mechanism, the facets,
the repetitive force of illusion—the jeweled speeches kept in memory

as he hammered the boards of the stage, hauled flats, swung one-handed
from the flies to set lights. Sometimes a person wakes up, sees he's meant
for another life—the snap-clasp of the theater trunk, high-voltage moving spot—

commoner, lord, poet: the armored breastplate. Sometimes he looks in
the mirror and sees no self but the invention, fathomable, fashioned—
the shapes of Art, all makeable—as in the machine, his machine,

                                    the machine that made him.

THE ILLUSION

After his death, I kept an illusion before me:
that I would find the key to him, the answer,
in the words of a play that he'd put to heart
years earlier. I'd find the secret place in him,

retracing lines he'd learned, tracking
his prints in snow. I'd discover, scrawled
in the margin of a script, a stage-note that
would clarify consciousness in a single gesture—

not only the playwright's imagery—but his,
the actor's, and his, the self's. Past thought's
proscenium: the slight tilt of Alceste's head or
his too-quick ironic bow; the long pause as Henry

Carr adjusts his straw boater; Salieri slumps at
the keyboard; Hotspur sinks into self-reflection—
where the actor disappears into physical inspiration.
Thought rises, a silent aria; thought glitters in the infinite

prism of representation. For love unrequited and tactical
hate, the shouted curse of a wretched son, a vengeful duke,
in that silent prescient dialogue—unspoken—he'd
show up in the ear, in a tone blue and sweetened as wood-

smoke, show up in these directions to the flesh: cues
like green shouts, the blood swimming with indicatives.

Look—the same smile he flashed at me
from the shaving mirror is here, right here—

but *realized:* I remember this path opening
in a deep forest outside Athens, the moon
shuddering into place—and no players as yet at hand.

PLAYERS

Every shadow spoke. They listened to the words
until they inhabited them, had them on the tongue
and in the brain, where we, who do not act, reside.

In that image-making niche, they appeared
to be like us: a simulacrum so perfect it hurt. They
could take us in and give us out like any other paisley

coat. We were, for them, keys to the obvious.
We were not the point, rather the point's point—
the arrow, flashing along its length as it misses

the target. Endless performance: it seemed
they were being applauded by the leaves of trees,
by the wings of birds. They painted big eyes over

their eyes, mouths over mouths. I understood finally
that deft imparting of momentousness: leaping keepers
coaxed out of plain words like sizzle from dull twigs—

sudden lit heartbeats—the hawk and the hawk's bait
flung upward again and again in the juggler's glove,
a naked woman in a claw-foot tub, your uncle, my uncle,

that crazy lion tamer with a busy head in Death's mouth.

The truth is neither simple nor clear
you say and everyone laughs because
this is simply and quite clearly true.
You are Algernon. You have been
Algernon before, though not tonight's

Algernon, not this exact cheerful anarchist.
Once again you have blurred identities.
Once again you have invented an invalid
who helps you escape convention and you
say the same things about him, differently.

Once again, you prove how insincerity builds
character, observe what a terrible thing it is for
a man to find out that all his life he's been
speaking the truth! The good ended happily and
the bad unhappily: That is what Fiction means, sniffs

Miss Prism—dizzy, dart-eyed as a pigeon.
Yet she has mistaken a book for a baby,
occasioning the play. By this error, she
has created character and erased identity.
You are Algernon. The importance of this

is carrying you forward, carrying you away.
We have a house—with mirrors, family portraits.

This is what Fiction means. Once again, we have
blurred identities. The importance of what is wild
and stays wild, untamable as truth, is to our

production, off and onstage, neither simple nor clear.

PASSPORT: A MANIFESTO

This is your passport I hold in my hand:
a hemisphere, half red ink, half blue—
as yet untorched by terror, but polluted

perhaps by the gaze of the future. For
example, the shadow of the parachute of
my desire, this rip-cord rip of your photo-

blink, your eyes translated into these
flashing sad idioms. Take this blank page
for the remainder, the last boring national

tattoos. *Wave me through* these invisible
brackets of lightning. Stars shatter on
the epaulets of all the uniforms, the hats

and coats of countries that no longer exist.
I wear your insignia, therefore I wear death's
insignia. Which means that nothing can hurt me.

And with these wings and flames, I pledge
allegiance to nothing: I can go anywhere.

That hot summer in London,
you were Ned Darrell. In South Ken,
we kept a bright flat, rented a paddle-

boat on the Serpentine, where you &
The Badger sat, moving. Galaxies spun,
swans drifted on their reflections. Up

from rehearsal, you kept on being him.
That far from you, I saw, was fiction.
At night, late, I'd lose myself in new chapters.

There—you stand at the mirror: Ned Darrell, worrying
his tie, gazing into my eyes through your reflection.
Murmuring about Nina in O'Neill underscript—what

the character thinks. Tugging at the silk knot,
frowning . . . *Isn't built to face reality, no writer is
outside of his books.* Then: *Got to help her snap*

out of this. I look out of the window, it's time
for you to go. *Help her snap out of this,*
I say, then laugh. But you look cross—

it's late, the car's outside. And see?
My own characters peer out of the mirror—
            the one you and he left trembling.

LATE KISS

On my study floor, the books were piled high.
You stepped over them, smiling, as you came in
to kiss me goodnight. The dog growled deep in

her throat. She loved me alone. You scowled at
the dog, then looked at me, the lit screen, the
stacked pages—and smiled. It would be hours

before I would slip into bed beside you, still
thinking about my book on life and death.
You always kissed me like that, late—

first pausing in the doorway. It was a ritual
you kept for years, begun after we'd settled in.
I remember our first night in the house—

I lingered in the room that would be my study. Bent
over my desk, arranging papers, I saw, in the corner
of my eye, a wavering figure in the doorway, half-perceived.

It frightened me then. Now I understand that it
came from the future, which has become the past. Now
I understand that it was you, smiling at me. You put out

your hand to ward off the bad dog, the mad guardian. She
growls again as I lift my face, distracted, still, for your late, tender kiss.

PORTRAIT

It is a portrait of a mother and daughter.
The mother is in a blue bathrobe, standing
behind her little girl, hands on her shoulders.

Once I believed it was a cocoon, the deep
colors spun around a gesture, half-indicated—
just begun to unravel between them. A flower's

slow bending down, petals falling: a release
of scent. But someone pointed out how tightly
the mother's hand grips the daughter's shoulder,

how threatening the dark trees—just beyond
the open window through which they gaze.
Why hadn't I seen through the suspension,

their seeming lassitude? They were alive,
not adrift. Why would life offer anything
other than its placid erasure? Nothing can last,

nothing will. Vines unfurl around the frame
in angry script, ominous branchings—where
the eye won't go willingly. Where did I

imagine the heart would go? To danger? No—
Past danger to dread, past dread to belief in
justice, past justice to refusal even of what's seen:

the elements, the future storm that writhes in
its own embrace, cloud-painted clouds. I would
ask to go back to the first moment when I stood

before it—I would ask to go back to the place
where the artist first understood something about
the shape we made: that far back, before inspiration.

BOX

Duke of Albany, clear-voiced, you, cursing
Goneril: *Not worth the dust the rude wind*
blows in your face . . . Then this hungry grief
seeking out your made-up natures. Left the room

as Captain Jack Absolute, Marat, Sebastian
and Fabian, Gallimard and Lucio: returned
as dust the rude wind lifts over the footlights.
Your box of faces. China white, pancake flat.

I peer into the oval glass embedded in the lid—
Zero there before anyone glimpsed your deft
threat. Mustache, spirit gum, grease pencil.
What peels from these too-solid imaginings of

your Self, this Prince Jester's pat laughter?
I re-trace lines drawn round the gathering
puzzle of aspect. Swinging grapes, rude wind,
stilled. That distance: first row to stage—

an unwrit page, you might have said. Your life-mask
kept in a carton: *Memento mori.* Yet you live
here in passion's glass—eyes watching yourself slowly
painting yourself, perfecting the inaccessible.

LE JAZZ HOT

At two in the morning, seeking nothing but air,
I opened the hotel balcony doors. It was there
in the distance, ridiculous, gorgeous: Eiffel Tower
under a full moon. Across the boulevard, the métro,
St.-Germain-des-Prés. There at the stop, a man
playing a saxophone, back to me, petitioning the moon.

What a used moment, a mimicry, I might have said to you
as you slept—though I swear I understood the importance of
what I was being shown. Never mind that his improvisation
offered choice after choice I could not follow. It was new again
and for what did I—did you—long? The painting or the package
of sabotage? Grief or ongoingness? Middle-nostalgia, but still, human
jazz: love or hate, go or stay—O the sax insisting: that dark averted face.

THE IMAGE

I turn on the television and he is
there, on-screen, in profile—
turning to stare full-faced at me.

A scripted wind lifts his hair,
he gazes outward and through me.
It seems he is a traveler, bored,

at a cocktail party on a terrace high
above a strange city. A beautiful
woman enters the frame, smiling,

throws her arms around him from
behind. It's clear now that he is
playing a happy husband or a lover.

He laughs again, gently extricates
himself from her embrace. That
woman holding him holds his life

in her hands, but his life is nothing
more than what he chooses to give her.
An exit line thrown over his shoulder.

A practiced emphatic smile. What he
chooses has in turn been chosen for him.
So later in the script, after they argue

in bed, she stares at the stripes of morning
light falling through the blinds across
his back and knows that he is only there

conditionally—and that the conditions are
not hers. It has been written long ago that he
longs to leave. Still, anyone with eyes could argue

the opposite. He longs to stay. Look at the
unspoken desire—the bands of light tightening
across the body even in its attitude of flight. The

tousled dark hair, the curve of the back, the
powerful muscles unresisting finally, the body
begging to be detained. Even though he sleeps

turned to the wall, she can imagine his
expression: the eyes wide open, perhaps
lit with expectation in that face he shows no one—

hidden from the lens, yet still an object of regard.

WINDSPRINTS

At that moment
we were both running.
Far away, you were rallying,
leaping up for the high serves—
I was practicing windsprints
            the next street over

from our house, our block.
Your racket flashed, you flung
away your cap. I can resist it:
the premise of coincident
speed and intent, but only so long as I can stand
the absence of context for our bodies. I need these to link us:
your quick wild laugh, your leap, the serve
exploding, the trajectory, my race with myself. I would

enlist the late sun also, linking us in its rays,
but then the terrible hand casts back, all the way back,
and the difference, unpent, comes breathing
up the white lines of the court.

MASKS IN RAIN

—for Michelle Latiolais

> A great while ago the world began
> with hey, ho, the wind and the rain
> for the rain it raineth every day . . .
> *—Twelfth Night*

Hey, ho, they crest the hill—in masks
with drums & horns & holes-in-stockings:
up to the White Horse gently piping.
Wren took ill but held the torch high,
Dobbs parried, swift in his torn doublet.

If the Lord Mayor grant a license to play,
there's hay for a bed. In the stalls at dusk
the lovers prompt each other. Ribboned corset,
farthingale. In rain, the new masks. A great while
ago, the world began. Began our kind: Dukes,

beggars, juggler-bears, heigh-ho as the locals
queue. Change into who-thou-wilt, into the stock
rovers, then the Old-Man-in-a Mask, the moon!
Change into a cloud that passes over the town,
the square, the little lit space where we speak

aloud in fans and tatters. Change into piss-in-a-ditch,
phosphorus flame and sword-from-the-scabbard, trapdoor
and gallows, dead child's face beneath the grinning mask—
Hey, ho, change! for the world began when the rain it raineth
every day.

THE CALL

When I heard the voice on the telephone
telling me there'd been an accident,
I repeated my question twice
without receiving an answer.

I was given another number
and at that number I asked again
without response. At last someone took
pity on me. That nurse in a distant blazing room

beginning to take shape before my eyes
paused, then put my question back to me.
Did I want to be told what was happening to you?
I looked at my daughter poised next to me, waiting,

her hand over her mouth. She inclined her head.
I do, I said, like a bride. And then the professional
voice, rising only slightly, called out to me, step by step,
precisely how your body failed—as she watched it fail

before her. I held the phone to my ear, repeating each
of these answers to my question, so that images of you,
disappearing, appeared in the air. Our kitchen, the dishes
in the sink, the stove, that shocked gaze meeting mine—

then yours superimposed over hers—your eyes wide
in that other room where you lay, rapidly dying
beyond the open receiver. The shouting technicians
hovering over your body as that other sound, unearthly,

spoke quietly beyond the monotone in my ear: blood
pressure, pulse rate, respiration. The soul, its heraldic
voice, murmuring other answers—then images, startled
one by one, from faith, from terror, from all that we
ever sought to know about you.

BUTTERFLY

The butterfly lands on my finger
and I gasp. The soul, the soul—
come back as a cliché of Nature!

I cannot resist. One wing is
tattered, the other whole: *my*
heart, your heart. Lord, I can

no longer live without messengers.
The psychic murmurs the words:
glass of milk, white sails, ruby ring.

My god-given capacity to dream—
have I given thanks for it?
See, the butterfly sits on my shoulder.

A new person, I connect hope & despair:
I connect nothing with nothing.

BLUE MORPHO

—for Bill Handley

We have only the Book of the Infinite to guide us
and how we interpret its unthinkable premise:
                              this life then an afterlife.

At the end of his, he saw blue.
I was told this. Eyes upturned
drawing the sky into one extended
                    remembrance of a present.

I was told this by the Reader.
In the depths of the trance she
cried out—foolish, a foolish creature,
but "gifted," as we say.
                    Familiar with the color,

for example, inside the chrysalis,
the bruises, doubling—how the morpho
divides itself in a hemorrhage of iridescence.

There is a reason why (deep in the trance)
his eyes blinked, as hers did,
and the wings, twinned, shuddering

stained with the color of the afterlife
                    opened before them.

VALLI

As she died, she became more beautiful.
That afternoon I saw her, near the end
of summer—she looked re-made, a pure echo
of herself, a voice thrown back from a great

distance within—but clear, resonant. She wanted
to live. Her hair had grown back in a shining
curve and her face revealed nothing of her suffering—
she looked young, expectant. But then, how else was

she supposed to appear, what else was she supposed to say
—drifting shyly into a silly party, every gaze on her?
That she was dying and afraid to die, that her life had been
made of leave-takings, that her breasts had been stripped away,

that her very name meant farewell? Now, when I dream of her,
she is speaking openly, enunciating, but without sound, like
the stray dogs she kept and loved. So many of them, barking
soundlessly, their voices extracted so that no one would complain,

no one would say that they were a nuisance. Now I wonder how
she found those creatures, how she tracked them down
in their illness and fear—coaxing them out of hiding,
persuading them to follow her into that silent animated world—

where she presided first as savior, then as one of them, after the knife.

ANNIVERSARY

Exhausted by pity, I sit
in the sun near the pool.
The wind lifts the chimes
you repaired so patiently

last year, knotting the strings
from which the silver cylinders
depend. The sparrow I brought
home in my hand outlived you.

The stray white dog insisted on by
the clairvoyant came home following Annie.
Eighteen years. The chimes shudder
into sound. How reiterative is pity!

How suffering stares at itself—
rehearses its strophic voices.
He was so beautiful, they say.
The widow sits with her white dog,

listening to chimes. *Eighteen
years.* The ring on the finger,
placed there by you. The ringing,
touching rings—your careful

hands tying the knots holding
this bright appeal in place. The
fixed listening of self-pity—so unlike
this pure sound, this consciousness

of you, setting the chimes chiming
that they might last a lifetime—
here where the ring re-inscribes
itself as a circle of wind anticipated

not that long ago by your binding touch.

LOVE SONG

Love comes hungry to anyone's hand.
I found the newborn sparrow next to
the tumbled nest on the grass. Bravely

opening its beak. Cats circled, squirrels.
I tried to set the nest right but the wild
birds had fled. The knot of pinfeathers

sat in my hand and spoke. Just because
I've raised it by touch, doesn't mean it
follows. All day it pecks at the tin image of

a faceless bird. It refuses to fly,
though I've opened the door. What
sends us to each other? He and I

had a blue landscape, a village street,
some poems, bread on a plate. Love
was a camera in a doorway, love was

a script, a tin bird. Love was faceless,
even when we'd memorized each other's
lines. Love was hungry, love was faceless,

the sparrow sings, famished, in my hand.

CHOICE

We each owed allegiance to a demanding god.
Your god asked that you attach to nothing, to no one,
but the illusion of choice. When, in fact, you had no choice—

you were the one waiting for invitation, always. Then you
were given lives to create, convictions. I too lived in that illusion,
writing poems alone in the middle of the night. Without choice,
there is no knowledge, she said. This was our reward for our godly

devotion. To hold up, at the end of one's day, the semblance
of free act. But the image failed us. We should have drawn
strength from this tradition, we should have been blessed, but
we were sentenced to keep entering that door, chosen, but opening on

the first set of revelations: the man's face and the woman's—
                                        on fire, impassable.

VILLANELLE

When you're beaten like that, you go away
she said, speaking as if he were present
though he'd stepped through the curtain, far away.

He was doubly lost then, because if she
was right, he'd learned early to check out:
when he was beaten like that, he'd gone away.

He told me the old man used a razor strap
and that strap split his back even as he fled—
even as he stepped through the curtain, far away.

He re-appeared in a column of light onstage,
he could be anybody, play any role they asked—
when you're beaten like that you go away.

Escape artist: the actor leaps through flames, snaps
chains, waves to the child from the taxiing plane—
then steps through the curtain, far away.

Far away: another role, a new cast of characters.
The intimate masks—The analyst offers hindsight:
When you're beaten like that, you go away.
He stepped through the curtain, far away.

OVATION

I try to make myself afraid,
the way you must have been afraid,
stepping out onto this stage—
but with a fear so pure, so

perfectly informed that you strode
out shouting. Here, where
the neon yellow arrows painted
on the floor shoot forward underfoot

in blackness—beneath the hanging
sequence of tinted skies—out toward
that mindless immortalizing light, now
dark. Now I think I feel the heat you

must have felt rising from the front rows.
A gaping fire door, a furnace:
your single body standing here
with no shadow, swinging on itself.

Had you been a fool, you might have thought
that they loved you. They never love you,
you said. They are hungry for the god
in his gold eclipse, the pure you on fire.

John and I move quickly, each with a handful
of ash, scattering. The sound of no sound falling
into the cracks in the boards, the footlights,
the first row. A small personal snow: a prince

of dust, a villain of dust. Each part you played
drifting up again, recomposing. I open my hand,
I let you go—back into the lines you learned,
back into the body and the body's beauty—

back into the standing ovation: bow after bow after bow.

EXTRAVAGANCE

High noon burns up the on-ramp
with that shifting, private glare—
one car, two, easing up to the green flasher.
(As he appears, stepping up now, striding

to the footlights for his soliloquy . . .) Just past
where I was—in the mirror—where in
the concrete wings, hawkers offer roses,
oranges, calculators. Elbowing out

the homeless, waving fast toward compassion.
(He lifts out of himself, a wave, not speaking
yet, but staring outward.) Everything deflected
here, lost or tossed off, gesture by gesture.

Crystal flutes of ruined grape, we lifted them—
afloat in the pool in the cliff hung over the sea.
Over the sea in that lavender-colored country.
He surveys their faces: a sense of growing

menace. (Then he laughs.) If you hit
the gas, you can shoot up the Diamond
Lane and merge into separateness. (*Calm
yourselves . . .*) He is reaching up now, as if

the words hang, pluckable, from the arc
above him. Profiles turning in the same
direction, rustling pages. (He knows
this house, having played it as a young

mendicant of the Muse. Tender-eyed,
then his sudden cold stare, gift of the old
man's wrath.) What is excess exactly? His
hand movements, the spin of gestures, memorized,

his body vibrating within the sudden rightness.
He begins letting the words out so that they
breach, cresting there before him, before
all who listen now. (What exultation

he must have felt when he first put foot
to accelerator, heading East from the West
Coast, a kid.) On location once in Kenya,
we popped out of the sunroof, photo-

graphing them eating the kill. The pride
slowly eating, then streams of running
zebra. Extravagance in all his expressions—
or nothing, locked nothing. He stands still;

the words fasten themselves to consciousness
from his breath. (He is a kind man, he says.
Then: *I will kill you.*) Born to burn money
in both hands, toss roses, those parade waves.

(*I will kill you* he shouts—and the audience
jumps, then laughs.) First-class cabin, vintage
bottles, view after view, a stream of zebra,
black and white sentences, unread. (*Your*

beauty lit by inaccessibility.) He would never
take liberties, he'd take leave, like Leone.
Looking for the exit now, right exit. The sky
afloat with portraits, he points to them. Then

the off-ramp. (*Look at your faces,* he cries,
then turns his back on them. Walks. The mirror
walking with him.) Over the speed limit, no stopping.
Turn off. A white banner is released above. Another.

All the hotel corridors, all the bars. No sound.
(He walks to the edge of everything, moving
outside the light's precinct.) Up the ramp
again, up the incline, where the figures wait

with signs and flowers. Give what you can, auto-
graphed stars, roses in cones. (He looks back.)
The applause, the furious working of eyes
to find him: shadow in the wings. The moving

light. The signs held up, the empty faces,
all, all, with a gesture of his hand, now related
$\qquad\qquad\qquad\qquad\qquad$ to each other.

THE QUEEN OF TRAGEDY

—after Catullus

Here she comes, the Queen of Tragedy,
dragging her train of black feathers . . .
Grieving publicly, grieving at the great
communal well. Tears, tears everywhere!

But Catullus' lover lost her pet sparrow
and that small moment fit grief perfectly.
The Latin: *pipiabat*—uncanny the precise
sound of the tiny bold piping—heard

no more. *In her lap or on her breast,
Her sparrow / lifting up like my sadness—*
cheeping all the time, hopping from one
shoulder to another . . . pipiabat, little incident.

Yes, in all the translations, it is a *small bird,
it is a pointless act.* This is what makes me
want to talk to you tonight, Catullus. You,
tagging the off-white walls with immortal

graffiti—making Lesbia's tears also eternal.
You eulogized the sparrow—bright-eyed
hopper on her breast, who inspired the great
sentiment—then flittered down the dark

alleyway of the Infinite. You did not flinch.
You'd rather have written of a drag queen,
of Aemilius' ass-breath, a botched campaign,
back-alley buggery. Anything but grief's needless

and sentimental acts, ridiculous forms—
from the tiny chanteuse whom she loved more than
her two eyes and more than you, Catullus—loved all
the way to tonight, this full moon in Los Angeles,

my sparrow asleep in her white cage, her lover flown away.
David dead. *Veil Venus* is what you said, veil the figures of
conquest in love, veil the image of love itself—for it mocks grief
in its swaggering, is that it? I want to know the difference between

love and grief—I want to know why we thought we'd live forever,
he and I—so unequipped for eternity with our bad jokes, domestic
strife. Caught between love and grief, the Queen of Tragedy
touches her brow, starts up again and everyone, Catullus,

I mean everyone, tells her to *shut the fuck up.*

HANDSEL

—for Michele Mueller

Hermes alone shall be appointed messenger to the underworld, where
Hades gives the ultimate gift and takes none in return.
            —The Homeric Hymn to Hermes (translated by Lewis Hyde)

Hand in hand became a handshake became a bride
beholding her first wedding gift. A step forward
then back as the word grew archaic: Archaic:

Initiatory gift—as at the beginning of a new year
or a new life. Knew a hawk from a handsaw,
knew what Hamlet knew, when the wind blew

southerly. *And stand a comma between their amities.*
Knew (or felt) the breath of the Messenger pent, but
I did not know this ancient word, set like a comma

in the red syntax of fruited boughs, the safety set
then spun on a handgun held to a sleeping head. Set
off down the road, silver coins scattered at the turning

year, new path, earnest penny, gift and business:
one breath between, one pause—but something more.
That contradiction I happened upon: a wedding-

chair in the graveyard. I'd first seen the word in my dream,
floating up—then was led to its reiteration: *handsel*
chiseled there in stone. Love and power, love and

payment, but all that too human in its evolving cost.
No, the gift here was of the underworld, of a perfected
hand reaching for mine. I sat on the bride side of the

throne, next to emptiness, the word in its carved blessing
at my feet. I thought I recognized the trick of no time,
an authoring I'd never known how to answer. Here I was

in a body, he in a soul only—and for a while I felt
married again in that place. I care nothing for the world's
disbelief, I care nothing for the invincible wind at my back,

though there was a hawk above me in the sky. See?
The eye seeks its connections, but this was more than
that, this was a message given in the name of gratuity,
given in the name of whatever pays for us, for these few heartbeats.

ELOCUTION

Stand still you said, as Donne might have.
You were an Elizabethan (by which I mean
you wore a velvet air of melancholy delight,
lute strings reverbing inside your laughter).

And your hoard of puns, far-flung as the
spheres chiming in consort—every image
you drew in the air stretched to heaven.

                    Stand still you said,
behind me in the mirror, your nimble fingers
at my nape clicking shut the clasp of my string
of garnet hearts: your gaze on mine, calibrated weight.

                    Like a merchant shaking out
gold-spun cloth, spilling vials of spice—
"Coffee?" you asked anew each morning, one eyebrow
                              up for emphasis—

                    Mimicking off-kilter
campy accents: Cockney, Canadian, French
cartoon cat. Donne, the great preacher,
was known for the "comeliness" of his pronouncing:

What was called the poweer of precellence. Advice
to actors-in-drag—to speak as neither passion's slave
nor a "pipe for Fortune's finger":
                              You stood, in

darkness or poured light—where "contraryes meet in one"—
the player and the poem blood-wed in Hotspur's tent or
                                        a penny pot of Malmsey wine.
Stand still you said. But I could not, could not

begin to pause at the shrine to stasis living makes of
us at times. Happy? No, but you could gird the earth
twice-round like Puck, you knew where the nightshade
                                nodded—

and when you sheathed your sword and reined down
the night-flier to your glove: in your quiet, all was quiet.
Though when I lay beside you I heard the music of your
                                        voice

beneath the sound of my heart all night, till the first light,
                        its sweet illlusion of everything on earth
                                        set in momentum.

FOR MARIE

The sparrows know it: the grass rises with it . . .
Tell me.
Who was I when I used to call your name?

—*Marie Howe*

Who was I when I used to call your name?
Sparrow? Finch? Like the two in their
white cage by the pool, arguing.

How we ate together, slept together, sank
into the distraction of distraction. Twenty
years. I have no memory of how we grew

into that familiar adversity, its diversions.
The sparrow, the finch—have everything
and nothing in common. He builds his

painstaking nests which she destroys
each day. He dances for her on the wooden
rung, hopping on one foot, then the other,

eagerly singing. She watches him quite
a while before swooping down on his banked
straw, his carefully woven threads and seed husks,

picking them apart so swiftly, one realizes
that what she feels most is a sense of symmetry,
an obligation—not even rancor, not even desire
                              to take something away.

THE EMPTY CHAIR

Your resemblance to Molière. There it was
in the cameo from your *School for Wives*
days—the same feral weighted gaze and
erotic mouth, playing out a small struggle

between flesh and spirit, won (in your face)
by the will to please—you could make your
smile conventional. But charm, rigorous charm—
how far can it take one? And the dangerous power

of impersonation. Actors give up their bodies
to it, their souls. Yeats quoted the Indian mystic
who said, *If a man died playing Hamlet, he would
be Hamlet after his death.* If I ascend on my last

breath to that bright stage, then behold you ignorant
of my face (or any other not in a mask)—could I
bear to love only a resemblance? All is resemblance,
within the swirling differing capacities. Molière,

onstage, feigning death then dying his own. His
chair left empty—like yours, here, black canvas,
director's style. Your name on the back writ in
the uncanny light that falls on what I've written,

each simpleminded coincidence. Then those
darker flashes of a larger portrait, the lineaments
of a criminal or deity, the argument of each made-up
gaze, Molière's likeness—or wait! Yours. Your face.

Romeo is a wanker you say—
and the other actors lift their glasses,
recalling grunting battles with Capulets
fought in battery-lit codpieces. Somebody,

cast as Richard Crookback, recounts popping
his air-filled hump, it shriveling like a balloon
on his back. Nobody ever wants to sing *"Try
to remember the kind of September . . ."* again.

Slick cads, kings, Hollywood whores, psychos,
all shot by the Messenger. The actors brandish
their glasses—what brushes against the glass
mouths is wind, slamming shut the skylight,

the lit trapdoor above that leads to heavens
resembling a parenthesis between identities—
where players wait to be cast. *Come night, come Romeo,
come loving black-brow'd night!* This is the space

between stellae—*take him and cut him out in little
stars* so that all the world will be in love with sweet audition!
The glasses float again, catching the great light, the Friar's
lifted philtre of fire, Juliet's eyes. Their voices rise in hectoring

chorus in the dreamy interlude before the coming acts:
                                   O Romeo, Wanker, Romeo.

CO-STAR

> Neither the sun nor death can be looked at steadily.
> —*La Rochefoucauld*

In the photo you embrace your
co-star, even as you were embraced
by that slow obliterative flame.
Your smile unfixed, unsubstantial
                            as smoke.

Not like the smile on the lips
of the man who strode up to me
that long-ago summer in the lobby
of a grand hotel in Florence—who

shook my hand, a little late—
with no apology, rather a perfect
expression of concern on a perfect
face: that blue matinee gaze.

That gaze relied on at once to
project anticipation, coming and going.
Energy and its divestment, like the pulsar,
collapsing into itself then outward. You

were always moving both toward and away.
Memory: your hand offered, mine outstretched,
your gaze meeting mine but simultaneously
drawn inward toward that separate radiance.

I knew even then that nothing stable
underlaid the world's foundation—

In my favorite chapel, Masaccio's Adam
and Eve wept and fled the Garden beneath

the messenger's familiar fiery sword. Death
itself a transparency within them now—but
newly visible—and what was that visibility?
Bones, red-lit through sun-drenched flesh.

Gold city of bones—martyrs, patrons—shadows
of palms. And these two: unwitting, reaching
out for the unbargained-for handshake, setting
something unseen in motion. Then outside a Vespa

starts up, another. Ancient light pours down over
              the Palazzo Vecchio,
                            and just beyond it, the beautiful bridge.

STUDIO CITY

The series of doors opening.
Through the last, a glimpse
of blue bedroom—

                    and beyond,
sliding glass, a pool in afternoon
sun. I glide through the doors

to you in the bed. I have flown
all day to visit you here on the edge.
We repeat that we are not ourselves,

or more ourselves than we could ever
have imagined: inane languid speculation,
new lovers. We have not asked to be

attuned, exactly. Something more
insistent claims our attention, the way
Nature here competes for the eye:

the glass doors open to pool and sky—
magnolia blossoms bend to hibiscus,
the raucous orange and red bougainvillea,

ridiculous birds-of-paradise bloom distracted—
How long can such extravagance last?
It's true. A far-off stubborn witness walks

within me, watches me sit on the bed,
touch your face. Watches the sun
unlatch, atom by atom, the outlines

of your shoulders and hair, watches
your hand as it glides over my lips, my
breast. *I will never grow old,* you say.

MAGNIFICAT

—for Leah

Her soul opened, but slowly,
a late bloom of thunder stirring
at the edge of the rainstorm. Then
lightning hissed across the stone floor

and she spoke to what stood there:
mirroring her, off-center at first,
then advancing across the threshold,
whole. Here was a girl pouring olive oil

from a stone jar into a cruet.
Pass through me into Time
were the words attributed
to her, later, when the nature

of the summons was clear. But
she'd said, *I magnify.* She was
with child and the child grew
into her answer. Impossible being

conceived first in her mind
as she poured fluid from one
jar into another. As the one
homely god poured rain onto

the dry earth and the other
writ larger and larger in the
pages of the Book, magnifying
her as the vessel, never the choice.

A PRIVATE MATTER

You, Never-You, the new vessel.
Dark/light of the sprung soul.

Flung upward or shuddered
up-ringing, iridescent as a fountain:

eyes flickering wide open in sleep.
And on the kitchen sideboard

backs of script-pages, cut up
by you to memo-size. If

someone jots a note, turns it over—
there are the words, dialogue of

people you once became or not.
Laura says she cannot command the

space station alone any longer, can't
he see this? Brent says he knows, he

knows what she has been going through.
I don't know what these words are for—

just as I know you will arrive no more
to counter this argument. You may

have said these things aloud. You walked,
you lay once beside me. Albert says suddenly

from a paper square: "Vague. Cryptic. Enigmatic.
Ambiguous." Claude says "How do you mean?"

I want to enter every semblance of you—
profile, ideogram, rainlight, zigzag kite,

shifting plinth. Even this comment
from Mohammed: "I should be going—

this is a private matter." Earlier, Frieda
has said "You're upsetting me, Ira."

Let me consider this private matter in anger,
in terror, in reverence. Voiceless, let me

consider a thumbprint, a top-sheet, margin
shout. Here's Marc crying, "Bullshit.

How can a man live in any other time but
his own?" At the tombstone, the fire pit,

at the anchor dragged brain-red over
consciousness, Yvan says, "I don't see why

I have to put up with your tantrums." In
this private matter, I refuse the lilac, the

anemone, all the lit banked candles.
Rachel says he's in the middle of nowhere,

without an alibi. Bring me no alibi.
Bring me instead one sprig, pale-white,

of your never-endlessness, one pulse-leap
inside the sick brilliant rose of your not-being.

Holden says "That's my girl." Fire-rose, ash,
drawn petaled, unpetaled, along my wall of

solitude. You hover, eyelit, at falcon-height—
and Serge cries, "Read Seneca!" Laura is alone

in the space station, weeping. I am not weeping.
I am emptying the pockets of my own monologues.

I am listening to the semblances, what you were,
who you've been. "You're disastrously open-minded"

a fragment says (it seems) to me, though I ask for
no feedback here in my space station, here in my former

life where there is no gravity—or this crushing gravity—
in my kitchen, my open mind. Where I listen closely to
                        no connections. To you, David. No you.

Disoriented, the newly dead try to turn back,
across the great expanse of water. But the distance
inside each of them, steadily growing, is what draws
                               them away at last.

Tenderness and longing lose direction, all terror
and love in the cells slowly dissipate.
                    Despite our endless calling,

their names fall away into the great canyons
of the infinite. They try to remember how to answer,
then turn away, distracted, from the repetitive cries.
                    What shall I call you now, lost sailor?

This was the port, this bright uneasy harbor where we never
completely set anchor. I understand the implacable clichés now:
"Its imperfection is its beauty" and so on. How instinctively we

defend the poor illusions of that beauty, the limitations of the present.
These colored paper lanterns are strung along our side because
we like the red-gold light, the pure ornament—

and because we insist on the desire of the lost to remember us,
to recognize the shape of our small flames. Late-night walks by
dull brimming water: candles and searchboats, bright beams scanning

for faces. Unstoppable need for solace, that hunger for the perfect
imperfect world. Still I sometimes think that you are too far away now
to recall anything of our side—not even that day we saw human forms

suspended over the sea: the hang-gliders at sunset, the old beach hotel
behind us and all our shining ambivalent love airborne there before us.

THE ROSE: 1984

Annie, it was the first full moon after equinox—and we drove after dinner with you asleep, to the new house where you will grow up. As we drove, your father and I sang along with a popular song on the radio, a sad thoughtful ballad about dying and being born again. A friend of his had written it and he described how she got it, word by word, then sang it piecemeal to her friends. Now it's just famous and people sing it without thinking, as we do when we know things by heart. For my part, I knew how he felt telling the story, thinking of the forming lyric, the steady resistance of the accelerator pedal under his foot, the cool wind ruffling up one side of his hair as he drove, as he remembered aloud. I suppose he felt me worrying without thinking, as I do, my foot against the floor on my side, braking out of habit.

We kept looking back at you in the car seat, your head rolled back in its sun hat, striped by the full moon, your dreams your own as you slept. Amanda's song on the radio, our voices joined then diverging into harmony and your steady breathing into a starry background you would inhabit only briefly, already bored with the fame of babies. The moon rising into the gold of its billionth pressing, the new moon inside it already an embryo—your infant dreams follow each other one by one, till they're all a single thing—like the melody still carrying us when memory suspends a word here and there. I try to remember how I felt carrying you, but I can only imagine it, a kind of fame—part of the well-known Ongoing, each little physical dream forgotten. But this—the moon rising, The Rose on our lips—completely sentimental the carrying of the tune—Annie, his hand on the wheel, the way he sang.

NOTES

"Valentine's Day, 2003": quoted lines from *Two Gentlemen of Verona,* Act I, scene 1. (The "speedboat" is mine.)

"Waiting For": quoted lines from *Waiting for Godot,* by Samuel Beckett.

"Not for Burning": a couple of lines borrowed here from *The Lady's Not for Burning,* by Christopher Frye. "Jennet" is the incomparable character Jennet Jourdemayne.

"The Importance Of": quoted lines from *The Importance of Being Earnest,* by Oscar Wilde.

"Strange Interlude": quoted lines from *Strange Interlude,* by Eugene O'Neill.

"The Queen of Tragedy": my rough translations of lines from Catullus' "sparrow" poems for his love, Lesbia.

"Handsel": handsel (or hansel), an archaic word I first saw spelled out in a dream, meaning a gift at the New Year or at the start of a new life: handshake, bridal present, coins, or gratuities. "And stand a comma between their amities" is from *Hamlet*, Act V, scene 2. "The Messenger" is the trickster god, Hermes or Mercury.

"Elocution": a nod to *Elizabethan Acting,* B. L. Joseph (Oxford University Press, 1951).

"Romeo": quoted lines from *Romeo and Juliet,* Act III, scene 2.

"A Private Matter": quoted lines borrowed from random playscripts and screenplays.

"The Rose, 1984": refers to the popular ballad "The Rose," written and performed by Amanda McBroom.

ACKNOWLEDGMENTS

I would like to thank the following individuals for their help and sustaining kindness to me as I put this book of poems together:

My former editor, Katie Hall; my new editor, Lee Boudreaux (and her assistant, Laura Ford); Jynne Martin; Danielle Durkin—and as always, my agent, Molly Friedrich. For close readings of the poems in manuscript: Sharon Olds, Robert Pinsky, Susan Wheeler, Cleopatra Mathis, Mark Doty, and Mark Strand. Thanks to Adrienne Rich and Billy Collins, and to Louise Gluck for the borrowed line and for wise counsel. I'm grateful to Lewis Hyde for invaluable and timeless advice about "the gift," Carl Phillips for help with Catullus and thoughts on ancient art, and Marilyn Parkin for "sparrow" lore. Thanks to Erik Jackson, Josh Rosenzweig, and Jason Shinder for encouragement. Lifelong thanks to my parents, my brother, Jimmy—and to Chris Abani: *baraka* always. Thanks always to Pam Macintosh and to Clarene Dong Rosten. And to my daughter, Annie, Bill Handley, Michelle Latiolais, and my sister, Michele Mueller—I can find no way to adequately express my gratitude to you; I can only offer (in the spirit of the "handsel") this heartfelt wave from the page.

And David, forever.